Interior Design Tips every realtor should know,
but doesn't

by Barrie Livingstone

68 interior and exterior design tips will change the way you handle listing appointments and clients.

After reading this you will never look at property the same way again.

Interior Design Tips every realtor should know, but doesn't

ABOUT THE AUTHOR

British born Barrie Livingstone is a self-confessed world traveling, interior designer and realtor who is fascinated by how we occupy our dwellings globally. Barrie came to the states as a teen. His early years were filled with an obsession of history and how we lived back then. Growing up he enjoyed walking through antique shops and old English Manor houses where he would revel in the charm and romance of yesteryear. He would imagine what it was like to live back then and how they acted in their homes.

So you can imagine the shock and the horror of being ripped out of jolly old Manchester, England at the tender age of 14 and plonked down into a brand new dry walled and peach stucco-ed Fort Lauderdale suburb. The house his parents rented by all means was a nice new home but to Barrie it was a nightmare of gigantic interior design proportions.

It was barren of style and robbed of the dignity that any home should be given, he thought. His new square drywall box of a bedroom was complete with this odd cottage cheese like ceiling. It was a 'tract home' on a recently drained swamp. To him this place was like the alien itself that came from the swamp. He would sit and lament and pine for jolly old home.

One day while shopping he found a very interesting crate like wooden box and a fantastic modern white lamp which his mum got for him. When he got home he placed the box next to his bed and then the white round lamp on it. It wasn't much as far as interior design goes but it was the only thing he could look at in the white sterile box. This is where I am sure his obsession with design and detail was born. Being placed into a white box at the edge of the everglades he knew there had to be more. And boy was there ever.

Years later he graduated high school and immediately attended the Art Institute of Fort Lauderdale where he graduated with honors and promptly moved to Miami Beach. He opened a design showroom called South Beach Design Group, with a partner and was designing for many clients. Here he was in heaven.

Realtors have been his constant friends throughout his lifetime as they hold the key to his new design business. After all realtors know who is selling and who is buying. Little did he know that one day he too would become one.

His entire career has been spent improving property whether it is residential or hospitality and he is now in his 28th year of doing so, a life-long passion that has now spawned 2 successful careers. Born on the passion of making property look, live and show its best. Barrie coined many phrases as you will read in the chapters ahead and one of his favorites is "presentation is 9/10th's the law". Presentation is everything and cannot be truer than when selling a property. The more you can do to make the property look good the quicker it will sell and for a higher dollar amount.

The following are 68 interior and exterior design tips that will change the way you look at property for the better. They are all things that Barrie takes for granted and so wonderfully shares with us on the pages ahead.

Barrie is currently Director, International Hospitality Development for Keller Williams in Downtown Los Angeles where he enjoys utilizing all of his skills on a daily basis. Selling off market pieces of land that will soon be the home of an apartment building and hotel requires a clear and precise vision which Barrie delivers to all of his clients.

For some reason he chose to write this in 3rd person. He likes the way it reads better he said.

Foreword

Take a look around you right now. Chances are you are in a room.

Look at the walls and the paint, the light fixture, or lack of one.

Is the door handle a nob or a lever, is it scratched or new?

Is the floor wood or carpet? What condition is everything in?

If you had to rate the room on a scale of 1-10 what score would you give it?

Don't hold back be ruthlessly honest.

I believe that every realtor has somewhat of a reasonable responsibility to have a certain knowledge of the basic items we all take for granted in and outside our homes. I stress it would be impossible for an agent to be in any way responsible to know everything, but having general working knowledge of how a property should present itself and how things are put together will go a long way when dealing with clients on listing appointments and in general being a good realtor.

Buying property in many ways is a liability as one never knows how much money a property may require once they own it. If you are buying a new home there is certainly less of a liability then buying a 50 or 80 year old home. We rely on inspectors for this to research and tell us things that we can't always see. However, no one can see inside walls and pipes. When a home appears to be well maintained visually it usually is. When a homeowner cares enough to keep a home super clean and updated the chances are the home will show and sell or rent quicker as a buyer or renter can see themselves easily moving in.

One thing is for sure, having the knowledge of these important design tips will help educate yourself and allow you to confidently provide your client with a much better service, which is why after all they chose wonderful you to represent them.

So with that said, enjoy the read and if you take nothing else with you but to learn to look around a property and make sure everything is clean, you will be one step ahead of your competitors.

"A room should be beautiful without furniture in it"

Barrie Livingstone

Being an interior designer for the past 28 years I live and breathe design on a daily basis. I have designed pretty much any space a human can fit into at this point and in many foreign countries. I realize that there are many things that I see and take for granted that I sometimes feel everyone should know as inherently as I do.

This is why I have the need to share with you my journey of design and hope that you can feel and experience space in the same way I do.

The following 68 interior and exterior design tips will change the way you handle listing appointments and clients. After reading this you will never look at property the same way again.

Why 68 tips?

There are literally 1,000's of tips one can give on this subject however 68 contains two important numbers that control Barrie's life. It also happens to be a perfect amount of knowledge to share for a first book and a sneak-peak into the mind of how a passionate designer really feels about property, space and the world of real estate

6 for creativity, both Barrie and Michelangelo share the same birthday, **March 6th**.

8 for eternity and prosperity. It also happens to be the year of Barrie's birth and a hugely important year **"globally speaking"**. Which is what after all Barrie does best.

1968

68 Tips starts here

No. 01 Paint comes in 5 standard finishes: **Flat, Eggshell, Satin, Semi-Gloss &Full Gloss**. It is important to know the basic characteristics of each finish and what finish to use where. Landlords of any caliber will much appreciate a nod in the right direction as painting walls in the correct, paint finish adds longevity and saves money.

No. 02 Flat Paint should only be used on drywall and plaster ceilings. It has no sheen and will not draw attention to the many defects and bumps a ceiling usually has. It's called gravity guys and what goes up on a ceiling facing down is definitely under the constant stress of being pulled off the ceiling. Often drywall and plaster ceilings will have bumps and lines, showing the poor workmanship of a drywall installer or the test of time and gravity being constantly pulled down. This is why the evil and very hideous popcorn and cottage cheese ceilings became popular in the 1980's. To save the time and money of greedy developer/builders they created this vile product. I believe that popcorn ceilings should be banned from sales and distribution and those installing them banished from the land.

Attention....**Flat Paint** is NOT wipe-able so should NEVER BE USED ON WALLS....EVER. It is my number one pet peeve as it wastes a client's money. It shows a painters complete lack of respect, dignity and knowledge of his trade. Walls painted in flat paint show every single, scrape, bump and mark and cannot be wiped clean. It can only be repainted. Walls that are primed and painted with eggshell finish or painted with a primer included in the paint are the best. They will be wipe-able and will stand the wear and tear of a years' tenant and beyond. When an occupant moves out walls can be wiped down with slight touch up at minimal cost to landlord/owner.

No. 03 Eggshell Finish Paint is loved by

walls the world over. If painted with a primer coat beneath or with an included primer, it will look good and last the through rigors of hectic modern day life.

Eggshell finish however, is not my recommendation for certain higher traffic areas. Narrower walkways 48" or less or any particular wall that is in a busy area, such as stairways or a foyer by the front door, kitchens or bathrooms usually need to be wiped down and cleaned more often. They may need a **satin finish** which has a touch more sheen than eggshell and it is even easier to wipe clean.

No. 04 Satin Finish Paint adds a really

stylish and polished look to walls. However, the wall needs to be as smooth as silk because there is slightly more sheen and luster to it so any imperfections will become more pronounced. Dining rooms, bathrooms and even bedrooms can benefit from the kind and gentle sheen that a satin wall finish paint provides. Additionally, smaller rooms can appear to have more drama such as powder, bath and kitchens.

No. 05 Semi-Gloss Paint is a fantastic finish

to use on doors and moldings if you want to pronounce gently yet not scream out "I'm shiny I'm shiny". I love to see a contemporary home have base boards, door jambs and doors all be painted in semi-gloss. It adds an ultra-chic look and can also be used in the same colour as the walls in the space. Back splashes, powder and bathrooms all can benefit from a semi-gloss wall finish, providing the walls are in good condition. The wipe-ability factor is majorly increased thus giving the paint job longevity.

No. 06 Full-Gloss Paint when applied

correctly is a true art. Sigh....I look to the famous front doors of my homeland in London.

The door to No. 10 Downing Street, home of Britain's Prime Minister, is my idea of complete and total paint perfection.

A smooth as silk, glossy enamel finish has been lovingly lacquered[1] on. Highly glossy and drenched in colour pigment, now that my friends, says style and confidence. Glossy coloured paint on a door creates a higher level of style and gives a building's entry dignity. Of course this divine finish also used to give us cancer as the paint had lead in it. Now we can enjoy full gloss paint that has no lead added. So if you're ever invited for high tea at No. 10, please avoid licking the front door on the way in, as the lead content is probably still very high.

---

[1]**lacquer** [lak-er]
  noun
A protective coating consisting of a resin, cellulose ester, or both, sometimes with pigment added. Best when sprayed onto a surface in a dust free room to give a mirror like appearance, free from bush strokes.
A resinous varnish obtained from a Japanese tree, Rhus verniciflua, used to produce a highly polished, lustrous surface on wood or the like.

Create inexpensive focal points in a home on a budget. Try painting moldings and doors in the same colour as the walls but in gloss. Moldings become more defined yet blend in. They will look chic and more expensive in a very Calvin Klein tone on tone way.

No. 7. Full Glossy Painted Front Doors

Front doors if not wood almost beg for gloss paint and please my dear friends do not be afraid of colour. We British love colour on our front doors, in large part because of the dreary grey English weather. A front door is the entry to the home and must be clean and well maintained. Wood stain should not be faded and sealed properly to look good.

Glossy painted doors, door jambs, base and crown moldings are a favorite and give us a feeling of security and establishment. Most gloss on trim is usually seen in a bright white and is also used on staircases, hand rails and spindles.

Gloss is easy to wipe clean, demands attention and therefore ideally suited for the outdoors and front door to a home.

The allure and mystique of a red door.

Feng Shui[2]laws say a red door attracts prosperity and wealth, so why not paint the bloody door red? Excellent alternative colour choices and depending on the style and local of the homes façade are: Black, blues, greens, oranges, yellows and purples.

The psychology of colour: The reason why a door should be painted in a colour is that colour draws attention to it. Our eyes will remain focused and keep being drawn to the colour. Colour affects our senses and when selling a home we need all the attention we can get and all eyes on the property. Have fun and tie in the existing architectural elements again (see curb appeal **No. 24**).

---

[2]**Feng shui**: *fēng shuǐ*, pronounced [fɤ́ ŋ ʂwèi]is a Chinese philosophical system of harmonizing everyone with the surrounding environment. The term *feng shui* literally translates as "wind-water" in English.

No. 8 Flooring

Floors take a beating! There as many types of flooring as there are surfaces in nature and beyond, to our now manmade world of synthetic look a-likes. To follow I have reviewed the most typical a realtor will encounter.

I myself am a traditionalist[3]. I prefer to use natural materials which as time plods on are getting more and more expensive. We hack down forests, carve up mountains and dig ever deeper into our poor planets core, all to make our homes look good. The need to have natural elements in our home probably dates back to times where we lived on the open African plains of Serengeti and in the caves of Northern Ethiopia.

We are obsessed with bringing the outside in because we love being outside yet need to feel comfortable inside our homes. Floors are the single most important element in a home or property as everything sits on the floor.

ASID American Society of Interior Designers [4] in their recommendations for design projects suggests that 25% of a design budget be spent on flooring.

---

[3]**traditionalism**[truh-dish-uh-nl-iz-uh m]
noun: adherence to tradition as authority, especially in matters of religion and in using natural materials wherever possible in decorating a home.
A system of philosophy according to which all knowledge of religious truth is derived from divine revelation and received by traditional instruction and perfection in home design

[4]**ASID American Society of Interior Designers** is a community of people driven by a common love for design and committed to the belief that interior design, as a service to people, is a powerful, multi-faceted profession that can positively change people's lives.

It is pretty obvious that everything in a home or building sits on the floor, unless one is selling space on Elon Musk's space-ex or Richard Branson's Virgin Galactica aircraft. So listen up and learn some flooring 101 basics.

We walk all over the floor! It is therefore important when preparing a property to rent or sell that we ensure that correct flooring is used.

Barrie's rule No. 1

"Use as few flooring types as possible in a home."

I cannot stress enough to you how disturbing it is to walk through a home that has 9 different floor types. I have seen as many as 36 (yes, I counted) flooring types in one major Malibu manse that has sat on the market for months.

Keep it simple. Main areas either in wood, stone or tile and if the budget allows, same in bedrooms. Please also note that cheap ceramic tile is what it is, and should only be used in low to mid income housing, never in what would be considered a higher end residence. I frankly think it is rude to use cheap ceramic tile in a high end residence and would rather see carpet so that a new owner can install what they like. Walking into a multi-million dollar home that has ceramic tile anywhere is NEVER appropriate.

No. 09 Wood Flooring has come a long way since the early school house, tongue in groove, solid plank days. Realtors today have to deal with what is existing and we all need to know the options as to how to make existing floors present and look their best.

The 2 main wood floor types we see are: **3" Oak strips in golden oak and Parquet Squares**

A natural no shine finish looks current   A shiny Finish looks dated

No. 10 Refinishing Existing Wood Floors has also evolved.

Most refinishing companies use vacuum sanders that vacuum the wood dust as they sand, thus leaving the jobsite much cleaner. Always ask for a company that has this vacuum option...trust me on this. It keeps the entire home clean and your seller will love that you took the time and effort to let them know about this option. It is now very standard to have wood floors sanded with the occupants still living in the home.

Dust is vacuumed away as its sanded

No. 11 Wood Floor Finishes should be non-shiny

at all costs as the trend is definitely towards matt or satin finish with no or very low sheen. Shiny glossy finishes are over and have been for a while. They also are the first to show wear and tear in high traffic areas as the glossy surface scratches then fills with black dirt that appears as black lines in the open wood surface. Nothing says dated like a yellowy shiny finish on a wood floor.

If your seller is having a hard time forking out to fix the floors, just show them the latest Restoration Hardware or Pottery Barn catalog and remind them how good their floors will look when the yellowy shine is removed. The new floor will look much more fresh and current

No. 12 Pre-finished & Synthetic Wood Floors

are all the rage now and some of them look very realistic and come in gorgeous shades of greys and naturals. The prices can be significantly lower than solid wood and the installation time is fractional, thus costing less money.

I have noticed that children, dogs and furniture can all do a number on these types of floors and often a full sand and refinish is necessary after a heavy use tenant or occupant. Landlords should remember that only 2-3 sanding's can occur on a pre finished floor as the wood is not solid. However, you should get many years use out of these floors and they look great and are easy to maintain.

The synthetic wood and vinyl wear super well and are basically a picture of wood that's placed on a wood grain vinyl. Great price and popular but not natural so not a favorite of mine. In medium to lower price homes this is very acceptable, but again I find disrespectful to use in a higher end home, as if you want to get top dollar for a high end home the finishes really do need to be up to par.

No. 13 Tile Flooring

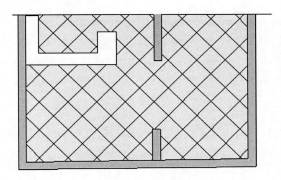

Urban Myth:" Tiles laid on a diagonal make a room look bigger"
Truth: "Tiles laid on a diagonal look cheap and awful and make one feel dizzy"
Barrie Livingstone

Basically, it is only permissible to install tiles on a diagonal if the tiles are a checkered marble in a period style setting or set as a tile rug in a small area. Otherwise, it is not encouraged to lay tiles on the bias[5]

Ceramic. Tiles are usually ¼" thick approximately. They can have a matte "preferred" finish or can be glazed in a shiny look, glazing often chips over time. It is easy to pop out a damaged or cracked tile as tile is laid on a thin layer of thin-set and held in place by the grout. Left over tiles can usually be found under vanities in bathrooms, pantry's or base cabinets in kitchens. Check garages and garden sheds as they are many times stored there.

---

[5]The **bias** grain of a piece of woven fabric, usually referred to simply as "the bias", is at 45 degrees to its warp and weft threads. Every piece of woven fabric has two biases, perpendicular to each other. A garment made of woven fabric is said to be "cut on the bias" when the fabric's warp and weft threads are at 45 degrees to its major seam lines. Bias here is used to describe the material "tile" being installed on a 45 degree angle.

Clay tiles such as Mexican Saltillo are popular, also terra cotta clay tiles. These are wonderful in the right type of home as many homes in warmer climates have Mediterranean architecture and Spanish, Italian or Mexican styles are popular. Cheaper clay tiles need to be sealed on both sides as when laid on the floor if moisture comes up from underneath a whitish bloom can appear on the tile and stay indefinitely.

Refinishing clay tiles. Are you aware that clay tiles are solid clay and can be sanded down, stained and re-sealed after many years of abuse? A favorite of mine is to do a dark tobacco rub or oxblood stain as it looks so rich. In kitchens and high traffic areas that have old worn finishes are easily sanded and should be sealed in matte non-shiny finish with a good grout sealer. The floors will come back and will show like new.

Mexican clay tiles are cheaper as the quality of the clay is different and the kiln firing temperatures are not as high as their Italian, Spanish or Moroccan cousins. Just as soil colour varies regionally, so does clay. Some of the most beautiful clay tiles found are paler and are Moroccan. They have a dull mustard and pale yellow appearance. I was in Jaipur, India where the clay is pink and the locals combine clay with goat yogurt to make a wall finish and tiles.

Tile size Always keep tiles as large as possible, it is the one and only thing that will make a space appear larger. When installing natural stone floors try to do a minimum of 18" x 18" and 24" x 24" as it really opens up a space. 12" x 12" tiles confine a space and in main areas reek of poverty.

Good tip. In most all cases tiles should be installed on the straight and the tile should be centered on the middle of the opening door into the space.

No. 14 Concrete & Terrazzo Floors.

Raw Concrete floors are fantastic because there are no grout or tile lines. They are a solid pour and are truly optimum at making a space larger. They should always be sealed in a matte sealer. I can't tell you how many places have shiny concrete floors and it is just not the look and will show scratches and wear in no time. They can be stained in natural colours and also painted for optimal command of colour.

Terrazzo is a favorite of mine for its sheer Italian genius and simplicity. Terrazzo is concrete that has marble chips as an aggregate[6] and can also have a colour added to it. Terrazzo was commonly used in the 20's and 30's in art deco buildings the world over, and is very much used in tropical climates. I was thrilled in my travels to see the row houses of Singapore and Malaysia using these floors. The marble and stone chips in the concrete keeps room temps cool. It was the perfect solution to use in art deco hotels as it can also be laid in intricate patterns.

---

[6]Aggregate aggregate noun: **aggregate**; plural noun: **aggregates**
A material or structure formed from a loosely compacted mass of fragments or particles. A whole formed by combining several (typically disparate) elements.

Restoration of terrazzo floors is easy. A large sander is brought in and then a polisher sets the sealer into the open porous concrete. These floors will last forever and should be treated with care and respect.

They are perhaps the easiest of floors to clean and there is usually several colours in the stone chips which make it fun to bring them out in wall and fabric color selections.

No. 15 Grout Colour & Width

Even its name sounds ugly.

Ugly Grout = Pig Snout.

I am not a fan of grout and never have been. Grout is rarely properly sealed and often made too wide and too dark, thus in my opinion ruining a rooms appeal. Remember to always keep grout line sizes as small as they can possibly be. Grout if not sealed becomes filthy, especially by toilets and in kitchens.

This basic ceramic tile is not happy looking at all.

This wide Charcoal grey grout is hideous and looks like a crossword puzzle on the floor; it would look much better if the grout were the same shade or a touch darker than the tile.

Grout when light such as this looks clean and better, and when sealed properly will stay light over time.

Shockingly True Fact. Male species urinate standing up and it splashes on floors to collect in grout... Ewh. It absorbs into grout. Yucky. Think seriously about what goes around the toilet and seal your grout accordingly.

"Good Hygiene is always in style."

Question time from the readers.

Barrie, why do we need grout?

Great question. Natural stone tiles are installed on a bed of mortar and are installed butt jointed (against each other) with no seams and therefore have NO GROUT LINES. The result is a clean looking floor that is easy to keep clean and is void of lines and ridges that grout lines have.

Grout is needed in between ceramic and thinner clay tiles as they are installed only on a thin layer of thin set. The grout actuality keeps the tiles in place.

Please remember that "luxury is not 12" x 12" granite tile with a 1" grout line". I never will forget walking into a **"luxury designer"** (I'll be the judge of that) model unit in Baltimore, Maryland several years back. The kitchen and bathrooms had 12" x 12" granite tile floors and walls with very wide, ugly grout lines in between. The sales literature was touting this as "luxury". It's like comparing Velveeta to a good brie, seriously?

No. 16 Grout colour

It is vital that grout lines should be just a tad darker or a similar colour to the tile itself. Medium greys and oatmeal's work well as they hide dirt.

Q: "What happens if the grout is too dark?"

A: "The lines take over the room and you will be living in a crossword puzzle, not a good look my dear."

No. 17 Natural Stone Tiles

are gorgeous and come in a range of colours and tile sizes. They are void of grout lines because of the way they are installed. Natural stone is from a rock so it is perfect to use outside and when used inside and out, near sliding or French windows, will give the illusion that the house is truly sitting on the earth and give a wide open feeling.

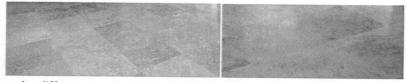

See the difference a direct butt joint looks on the right vs. the wider line of the left side. Over time grout will also discolour.

No. 18 Porcelain Tiles

have a remarkable life-like resemblance to stone. They are thick and heavy like stone and require the same installation as stone, therefore eliminating grout lines. The best benefit of porcelain tiles is that they do not need grout and are installed butt jointed.

No. 19 Carpet (wall to wall) is my least favorite type of flooring as it holds in all the dirt of the day, the week, the months and the years. If you only knew how truly filthy, disgusting and unhealthy carpet is, you would never want it near your feet or lungs.

I spent 2 years living between Dubai and Malaysia and on that side of the world wall to wall carpet is NOT used residentially at all. Filth and allergens are not good for anyone's health. However, if you must use carpet here goes some tips... well you know I am not getting any carpet sponsors from this but I must be honest.

There are a few carpet types such as commercial patterned loop and the classic wool ax minster that I adore. In hotels due to sound issues, we really rely on carpeting, but please know that in general carpet by its very nature is filthy and unhealthy.

There are 2 types of carpet most commonly used and they are known as **Cut pile** or **Loop**.

No. 20 Cut Pile Carpet has the fiber sitting vertically so that when you walk on it, it's very Cush n Plush. It feels soft and nice underfoot and many love it in bedrooms. Wool and solution dyed nylons are the most popular fiber types used. One must be aware of the "off gassing" and the chemicals used that we inhale. When you smell new carpet you are inhaling poisonous toxins. Yes sleeping, watching TV, eating chocolate and having sex on poisonous toxins.

There are now many green carpets we can use that will not Off Gas and are healthier alternatives. The inherent nature of pile is that it feels good to walk on as we walk on the ends of the fibers. However, in certain areas is also its downfall, because we are walking on the tips of the fiber in higher traffic areas such as doorways, halls and stairs, as these areas are the first to show wear as the pile smooshes down over time. Here is where the Loop comes in to save our day and our pocket book, especially for rental properties.

Loop and **Cut Pile** are easily identifiable. Guess which one is which?

No. 21 Loop Carpet is exactly that. The fiber is

knotted in a loop so one is walking on the sides of the carpet fiber. It is many more times resilient than any pile and perfect for longer lasting higher traffic areas. All commercial carpet is loop; Combination patterns in cut pile and loop are wonderful as they are rich in both depth and colour as you see the top and sides of the fiber.

The oh so common **berber carpet** has large loops so it can be cleaned more often and lays flat to the floor. It is usually made from an olefin fiber that can take many steam cleanings. I believe berber carpet is probably more vile and cheap looking than any popcorn ceiling and it reeks of poverty. It should never be installed. If you have the ability to intercept its purchase from a seller please remember that a great alternative is a low pile commercial loop. Very inexpensive and it can be glued down directly to the floor for a smooth finished look.

No. 22 Carpet over Padding or Glue-down Method?

It is important to know that carpet padding is an excellent sound absorber. In bedrooms on second or 3rd floors it really helps absorb footsteps and general household noise. It should also be noted that the thicker the pad the less time the carpet will last in higher traffic areas.

In commercial and rentals always use a **glue-down** directly to the sub floor or a lay carpet on a thin felt padding so the back of the carpet is less stressed and will perform longer and show less wear.

Q: "Barrie, why does carpet padding shorten the carpet life?"

A: "When the pad is thick, as we walk on the carpet the back of the carpet weave gives in and moves. Over time the fibers break down and the structure of the carpet becomes weakened."

No. 23 Natural Fiber Carpet

Sea grass, jute and coir have been in and out of home fashion since the mid 90's. Be wary of installing this product as it is the MOST temperamental of all carpet flooring. Natural fibers like grass and husks have a natural smell to them, so non-well ventilated rooms will definitely take on an odor.

Stains, anything that drops on it will likely stain it. Even water will stain as the fiber soaks it up and will take a while to dry out.

Comfort, most of these carpets are very rough under foot and are not nice to lay or sit on. If you like this look then I would turn to some amazing man-made products such as Sisal-tec by Karistan which provides you with a gorgeous soft and durable alternative to coir with all the warmth but none of the stain worry.
They also come in some nice greys and silvers, a very sharp look.

No. 24 Staging a Property for Sale or Lease

When staging a home for sale, all senses should be addressed. **Vision** and **scent** are both as important. If a room or home has a bad smell, it is an immediate turn off. Windows should be opened as nothing beats the feel of fresh air in a home. It's a good idea to leave scented air fresheners in a few places so that a home smells inviting at all times.

Staging is to help a buyer see where certain activities will happen. Remember that less is more. One should stick to regional favorites when staging and also be house appropriate when selecting a design. A Malibu Beach House theme in a Victorian home in Virginia would not look good. Artwork is important so walls are not bare as art is at our eye level. Books and accessories make a space feel lived in.

In areas where a house may sit on the market longer, I recommend buying furniture as it is surprisingly affordable. I recently staged a 2,000 sf 3 bed/3 bath home on a $10,000 budget complete with all artwork and accessories. The clients were about to spend $5,000 on the staging for the 1st 30 days then encounter monthly fees.

The furnishings are a tangible asset and can be either sold to buyer or used in another investment property, as was the case for my investor clients. Either way the money was used to buy a tangible asset.

No. 23 Showing a Property

Always arrive at a home showing a minimum of 15 minutes before a client's scheduled arrival, depending on the size of the property, as each space is different. I had one 14,000 sf home in 3 buildings that took 2 people a minimum of 45 minutes to open up.

Time yourself, presentation is everything and can make or break a clients' opinion of a property. Open windows a bit, all window treatments need to be open and every light should be on. Open all doors to rooms except closets and storage rooms. When it is your listing always make sure that you keep certain items like toilet roll and air fresher in a bathroom.

If a house is vacant make sure owners send the cleaners in to scrub everything clean. After a month it will be necessary to have another light dusting. Always walk through your listing with a keen eye, as if it is your first time in the space so you notice smells and cleanliness.

Make sure you keep bottled water in the fridge as it is always a good idea to keep your clients comfortable and well hydrated so they remain alert enough to make a purchase.

Outside areas have become increasingly more important to buyers, so whether you're in San Diego or Cleveland make sure you always walk around a property and into the garden or yard with clients.

"When you buy a property, you own it in its entirety!"

Walking a client into a garden and onto a lawn or by a pool gives them a sense of the place they may well own. Allow them to feel and experience a property that they may very well be owning one day.

No. 24 Curb Appeal

"Presentation is 9/10th's the law!"

A first impression is everything! It is vital that a home looks its' best from the street or main approach. When you take care to notice every detail on a home, it shows pride of ownership and gives a home its value and dignity. Even in markets where homes fly off the proverbial shelf a home should always be treated with respect as it is the most costly item a person will buy.

Would you go on a job interview without brushing your hair or teeth? (if you say yes, read no further)

Would you put on your best and most appropriate outfit to meet a new client?

So don't think of putting a home on the market without taking an assessment of how it presents itself from the curb.

No. 25 Exterior Lighting Fixtures

Make sure they are clean, free from dust, cobwebs and birds' nests please. I am shocked at how many really nice homes have dirty, old small light fixtures outside the front door.

Typical homes will only have 3 fixtures outside them. 1 at the front door and 2 aside the garage doors, so make sure they look new or buy new ones. Pay attention to the style of the home and size of fixture. Don't be putting no Spanish style iron on a craftsman style home as you will kill the vibe.

We live in a time where we can shop by style and price for items on our phones and have them sent to us rapidly so there is really no excuse.

Old, rusted, filthy & too small vs. New, clean, stylish & great size

No. 26 Front and Garage Doors Let's hose

and wipe them down please so they look clean and in good condition. If they don't look brand new paint or stain them. This is the SINGLE most important thing to do that is almost free. Avoid the white garage door if you can, unless a home is cape-cod, colonial or a cheap cookie cutter style.

Somewhere deep in the "SBTHBAA" **Suburban Bible of Tract Homes Association of America** it is written. **Psalm 21: 2.** Garage door "and the good lord said unto us a white garage door shall guarantee you entry to the pearly gates".

A huge wall of white sticks out like a sore thumb. Many times I recommend painting the garage door the same colour as the home's walls. It will disappear miraculously and automatically look richer and make the house look different.

Don't you think if this door was painted in a painted in one of the colours in the brick or in wood that it would look richer?

Wood Graining a standard aluminum garage door to match a front wood door or windows adds a huge value to a home as it looks like a pricey wood door.

White aluminum Doors can be faux finished at a fraction of the cost of real wood garage doors.

No. 27 Door Knobs & Handles

Make sure all door hardware is clean. Hinges and inside door jambs should be wiped clean and be in working order.

Make sure if you have brass accents then all fixtures are brass, it will make a statement. If you have black iron lights and black iron knobs it will clearly look better than that pitted old chrome one that's there now.

Keeping all metal on a home's exterior the same finish will make the home look its best.

Pitted old and sad looking Home Depot special circa 1982

My absolute favourite is Rocky Mountain Hardware.
This doors got style baby!

No. 28 Mail Boxes

should also be clean and if possible make them a style that goes with the exterior of the home. Mail boxes should be fixed to a wall or on a post as per local post office codes and not be loose or falling off. Typically mail boxes are black metal. A very easy "look new" fix is a good wash down. A light sanding then spray of black iron paint on the box will make it look new.

If the box is at the foot of the driveway it is nice to accent the post with some greenery or low shrubs. Avoid or remove anything gimmicky. Driving round suburban Florida I've seen my share of concrete manatee, dolphin and mermaid mail box posts. Not a good look at any time. It is better to have a plain simple black metal post... promise.

No. 29 House Numbers One easy way to make a statement and give added style and great street presence is to find some fun numbers for a home. Remember to be true to the homes architectural style, even if it's a cookie cutter track home there usually is some essence of style the developer tried to give it. Work with what you got and make it something to look proud of. So whether it's Mid-Century, Tudor, Cape Cod, Modern or Mediterranean there are a number of styles that will match. Look online and you will find the perfect ones for the house. Try typing in "architectural house numbers" to see the many available styles. If all else fails, Home Depot has basic black or brass numbers.

Oh, one last thing. Please make sure to install them straight. By drawing a light pencil line on the surface that should be easy. Also, don't get the numbers so small that the mail man and your guests need a telescope to see them. Remember, people use house numbers to find a house and many times numbers may be the first impression a person gets of the property.

Architectural numbers give clean modern look and are perfect for mid-century or modern homes

Hand painted numbers add a touch of romance and hominess

No. 30 Driveways, Paths & Walkways

should be free from debris and if there are any loose bricks or stones make sure they are put back in place.

Power washing is a great idea as it removes dirt build up and makes concrete and stone surfaces look newer again. Depending on the type of material used sometimes a light matt sealer will add dimension to the surface and again bring it back to life and make it look well maintained.

Walkways and paths around the sides of a property or in a rear garden should also be free from any debris and walkable.

Remember buyers are buying the entire property and the more buyers see of a property the more value it has to them.

Attractive pathways create style around a property

No. 31 Lawns & Landscape.

Nothing should be dead on the property. All branches or tree limbs should be removed and trimmed along with anything dead or dried up.

Try color spotting key areas with either seasonal flowers or year round native grasses or shrubs that will accentuate walk ways and under windows.

Always use native species as they will require less water, look better longer and are good for our planet.

Guess what guys? Before your house was there it was earth in its natural form so let's remember this and not use grass if we are in a desert…. Seriously?

If you are looking for not only perfect Architecture, but perfect land and hardscape. Look no further. This home below is perfection.

The Kaufmann House by Richard Neutra in Palm Springs. Note the carefully placed desert Rocks interspersed with a variety of native desert cacti and other succulents, which require no water.

No. 32 Hardscape & Retaining Walls

or any brick or concrete walls should be power washed and cleaned unless you are selling a historic property with ivy and moss growth on the old stones or bricks. Cracks in walls can mean problems so try to cut out and redo small parts of walls to present better

Many times water intrusion makes paint on retaining walls bubble and peel. This is not an acceptable look as it screams to a buyer "water leaking through". Sanding and sealing with a professional sealer and paint is the only way to remedy this. If there are too many walls and expense runs too high at least make the ones in the front of the property look their best as curb appeal rules.

Wood fences should not be missing any panels, if they are fix them, sometimes a few nails can help secure a loose piece of wood, and sometimes a new piece is needed. If the stain on a wood fence is faded and looks bad it is probably best to have it re-stained and you will see the magic as it comes back to life and defines the property.

A cracked retaining wall showing obious movement of earth looks menacing.

A stone clad retaining wall with steps adds a welcome feeling and great style to any property

No. 33 Roof Tiles. If a roof can be power washed it will look much newer. In areas where there is a lot of precipitation many times moss and fungus grows on roof tiles. If the home is not historic it is not okay. I'm not sure how this became an acceptable appendage for roofs but I find it un-nerving to see slime and organisms growing on a roof, unless of course you are in a Harry Potter style Gothic or charming original Tudor.

Fix any loose or damaged roof tiles as that's a tell-tale sign that the roof may be in need of a major repair.

No. 34 Gutters should be clean, painted and fixed properly to the home. In general gutters should be painted to match the fascia on the roof or wall so they seem to be invisible, and gutters down walls should be painted the same colour as the wall.

A great trick I use on homes is to order the aluminum gutter in brown as it looks like aged metal or copper and is a fraction of the price. I have used real copper on the front of homes and the brown aluminum on the sides and rear. No one would ever know... besides me of course, because I look for pigment discoloration on the sides. If there is discolouration in a few colours this means its real copper.....lol

**Copper gutter (left) will age and go brown very quickly.
Brown Aluminum will remain brown**

No. 35 Chimneys should be free from soot stains at all costs. When the fireplace damper is blocked or something is wrong with a flue, a black sooty chimney is a dead giveaway that there can be a problem. Ensure that the damper at the top is secured on and straight please.

Decorative chimney caps really add character and provide an excellent focal point architecturally. Their presence on a chimney pronounces the home as one that has significance and that the owner and builder took pride in noticing the details.

No. 36 Window and Door Shutters can

make or break curb appeal on the front of a home. Clean and intact shutters are a must. Did you know that you can easily measure the shutter and order new ones at a cost of $55-90.00 each and they come either paintable or in colours. They even come in a wood grain plastic that you cannot tell is not wood from a distance.

So why then given this, are there so many ratty, cobweb covered, cracked and sad looking shutters out there? Did you know that the wicked witch lived in a home that had shutters falling off?

Wicked Witch house on Camden and Walden, Beverly Hills, California.
Just a short walk from the shops on Rodeo Drive

Q: Would you like to live in the wicked witch's house?

A: Yes, but only if it was the original one from the wizard of Oz that is in Beverly Hills.

Did you know that shutters are supposed to actually look like they are functional?

Anyone who has visited the Italian peninsular knows that the opening and closing of window shutters is at least a three to 4 time's daily ritual. First in the morning to welcome in the sun and fresh air, then close after lunch for siesta, then open to catch an afternoon breeze, close for bed. You get it. Shutters should look operable.

Mama Rosa Perino. Portofino, Italy

Ensure that the shutters are fixed to the wall as close to the opening of the window as possible. If there is a large frame around a window, it was not meant to have a shutter and will look silly with shutters stuck on the wall beside the frame. I am surprised both residentially and commercially how many people enjoy sticking plastic shutters on buildings and think that it adds nutritional architectural value to a property when it actually looks comical and clown-like.

Shutter accessories are fun with the right style home. Cape Cod, Tudor, Spanish or Mediterranean can all benefit from ordering decorative flat metal hinges, handles and clavos[7]. They add a touch of authenticity to a building's façade and help make the shutters actually look functional, which in turn adds charm and age to the home.

A rustic iron Clavo   The charm and old world feeling of real wood shutters is second to none. Please note the hinges are placed as if they can actually be closed and opened.

Although these handsome blue shutters have been correctly installed flush with the line of the window they are missing the hinges. They do not look like they are operable and look like they are just glued on. This is a perfect example of what not to do.

---

[7]Clavos. (Noun) Clavos is the Spanish word for nail or spike. It is used as a rustic decorative element on the exterior of building components like doors.

No. 37. Window Boxes and anything that's fixed to the house should be clean and fixed properly to its surface. The idea is that nothing should look like it has not been maintained, to a buyer these are tell-tale signs of differed maintenance.

Window boxes on certain style homes look gorgeous. They look gorgeous when the red geraniums are full and cascading in abundance down the window sill. However, window boxes with dead or lifeless plants in them are more of an eyesore. Stick with simple boxes and make sure that there is a plastic lining in all boxes. This keeps the water in so you don't need to water them so often and prevents water from escaping and dripping down the wall and thus leaving dark streaks, like the eyes of Tammy Faye, god rest her darling soul. Not a good look

"The Eyes of tammy Faye" Worlds of Wonder Production

Ferns and shade loving plants for north facing or covered windows where sunlight is not direct

South, east and west facing windows can have full sun flowers.

In hard to water areas or arid places like the desert southwest and California I like to see a succulent garden as they love to be dry and can take water only once a week or two depending on the level of full sun.

Seasonal window boxes have a major impact on a buyer, especially during autumnal and holiday times. Try adding small squash, pumpkins or gourds during November and December showings, add poinsettias or a splash of red.

No. 38 Fences, Walls & Hedges surround

a property and keep it enclosed. They define a property's boundaries. Like a moat around a castle or a wall surrounding an ancient city. Walls, fences and hedges need to look like they proudly surround, protect and define a property, not look sad and mistreated.

Walls: Take a hose and wash down painted stucco, brick or stone walls. Did you know that stone and brick walls can be painted with a clear masonry stone sealer in of course a matte finish which adds depth and luster to the wall and gives a more styled appearance. That's of course if you're not going for the big bad wolf house; In that case keep it looking dirty so only the little pigs will come by for tea.

Hedges: If hedges look like they have mange and have gaping holes in them, then do a deep fertilization treatment, water often and cut lower if necessary. No use having a 6' hedge that's holier than a slice of Alpine Lacey Swiss. It is far more appealing to see a trim and full 3' tall hedge that looks healthy.

A beautiful healthy looking well-manicured hedge

Fences Fix any missing planks or replace any fence boards. Fences also need to have the same stain or paint all around. If there is NO budget to fix a rotten wood fence it may be necessary to remove it all or just replace a section. See the difference below.

Property Boundary Lines: One of the most frequently asked questions whenever showing property is a very simple "Where does the property end?" Many times a small or low hedge can be planted to give privacy or delineate a property boundary. This can also be done with larger boulders or rocks.

If there is no budget then it's a great idea to place at least a stick or something at the end of the yard in each corner so at least the property lines are clearly defined. Clearly boundary lines must be referred to a survey but it's nice to have some idea of a property's boundaries.

Neighbors and Boundary Lines: Always consult with neighbors and ask their opinions on any matters that about their property. It is better not to surprise them. If someone placed a hedge or fence suddenly in your wide open back garden you would be a little shocked. Common courtesy dictates that a nice friendly chat can go a long way, providing they are not insane or rude. In which case I wish you luck.

If your neighbors share the same boundary line vision as you do, you may even get them to pitch in, as it is along their property line.

If you are not nice to your neighbor, you would not want to wake up one morning to this charming hedge installation, would you?

As always make sure a licensed fence company that uses a surveyor puts the new fence or wall in. If it is placed on the wrong side then in years to come it may become a problem and have to be moved.

If a property is neglected on the outside, then lord only knows what is going on inside. Boundary fences, walls and hedges are an important part of any property.

No. 39 Interior and Exterior Walls.

Anything that is on a wall that is not painted should be clean and well maintained. Often walls have tiles, wood paneling, shelving, stone cladding, niches etc., wipe clean and ensure that whatever the surface, it looks its best. If there is damage it is many times best to simply remove and properly paint the walls.

Walls are in our line of vision and when they are poorly maintained a buyer will notice. Cracks in cement and stucco are signs of a house settling. In certain areas it can mean damage from earthquakes and send alarms off to a buyer. Please address all cracks as any inspector will find them for sure.

No. 40 Molding

Molding, Molding we all love our molding.

The great love affair with molding often makes people in Middle America Land do things that are NOT in the best interests of a home.

Pet Peeve number 7,068 is the almost obsessive & compulsive behavior of people from the South or Texans who must have chair rails in their tiny dining rooms or hallways that have a standard 8'-0" ceiling height only. Too much going on as the rail going horizontally chops the room in half and makes a ceiling appear even lower. What is worse is when they wallpaper or paint it a different color below the rail.

Does this look nice to you?

It's better to have a plain painted wall, free from the distractions of wallpaper and molding. Don't you think?

Chair rails were installed originally to protect walls from chairs that were placed against them and then later in great homes for decorative purposes. How a fake foam 3" rail ended up becoming a staple in cookie cutter homes is beyond me. I would strongly advise putting money into a better chandelier my dears.

The crisp clean look of this flat molding is inviting and gives the room a sense of style.

White molding Heaven

Make sure that moldings tell a story and they all match. Even if a home has only base and door trim they should all be the same size and painted properly (see item No. 01). Higher base than a standard 3" is always welcome. A favorite of mine is to always go with a minimum 6-8" bas board trim as these really do define the room. I also love a minimum 4" door surround molding as it makes the door stand out.

Builders 3" molding is just that and is a basic standard. If a budget permits you to switch out 3" door moldings then please do. You will be very surprised that these somewhat permanent looking moldings come off the wall in literally a second with a hammer and chisel.

The new wider moldings are typically pre-cut outside the house and brought in to install. I ask my painters to paint the first coat so that the time it takes to put new door molding in is very minimal.

The result is amazing as doors really do provide architectural presence in even the most cookie cutter of spaces.

No. 41 Interior Doors

Doors are the entrances to rooms, providing a place for us to enter and exit. Doors should always be painted properly and have working hardware.

In dark hallways and areas that have no light it can often be a good idea to have a French door that has frosted glass panels in it. These allow natural light into a room if there is a window in one room and not another.

The single lite frosted glass door allows light to filter thru while still keeping privacy and is a great addition to many rooms

There are so many door styles and types that one can write a book on them alone, but the basic concept for making a home look good is that all the doors should match.

Front doors and rear entry doors can always be different and it is very acceptable to add doors that have glass panels into the mix, as long as they are in keeping with the homes existing architecture.

Uniform Door Styles Please keep doors the same style. I cannot tell you how many 4 bedroom, 3 bath, 3 door type homes I have walked into. Doors should all match, if one is paneled and they are all flat it will stand out and not look good. Unless there is a need to allow light to enter into the core of the home. Allowing natural light into all spaces is of paramount concern for any dwelling.

Bi fold closet doors are perhaps one of the worst inventions ever. The ones with the louvers actually scream tenement. Whether aluminum or painted balsa wood they are flimsy and many times cracked and broken.

My recommendation is to keep these types of doors flat. It is acceptable to use hollow core doors as they are much cheaper and are okay to use if you are moving out. However, if you are moving in I always recommend a solid core door. Not only does it feel heavier and more important it has a much better sound quality rating. For toilets, bedrooms and laundry rooms it will keep noise inside and allow for more privacy in general.

Cracked or missing louvers are not a design trend.
Unless you are a peeping Tom.

No. 42 Hinges

Pet peeve No. 6,087 is painted hinges. I am a firm believer in painted hinges being outlawed and severe jail sentences for those who paint hinges, as they look cheap and tacky and completely ruin a look.

Hinges are really inexpensive and any odd job man can change them in minutes. By keeping hinges the same colour and finish as door hardware (which should also be complimentary to the homes other metal finishes) what you are doing is branding a theme throughout a residence. A theme that will appear to the buyer as well thought out and feel upgraded and expensive.... ssh don't tell them.

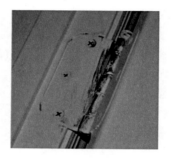

You would be surprised at how many homes have hinges painted in this vile and sloppy manner

A new hinge costs a few dollars and gives the appearance of new construction, freshness and looks like a home you would want to live in

No. 43 Door Hardware Little known fact No: 4,632.

The average home will have around a dozen or less doors. Yet I so often see a brass handle and a chrome knob in the same residence and always ask "why?" door hardware all needs to match and when it does it cohesively creates a home's design. Finishes should tie into lighting and other knobs and metal objects in the home that are attached.

Door hardware is easily changed and adds a subtle yet rich architectural element to a home and I would say an important one. Nice knobs and levers can be found from around $30-100.00 each and if a home only has 8 main doors are well worth the investment.

Set back and door thickness. These are the 2 things you will need to know when ordering your knobs.

There are really only 2 sizes of door thickness and they are 1.25" for interior and 1.5" for exterior and set backs are 2.25 – 2.75". Many standard are adjustable and it is very easy to measure how thick the door is and how many inched the center of the knob is from the edge of the door.

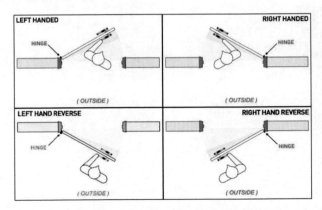

If you are ordering levers you will need to know if they are left or right handed. See the above diagram.

No. 44 Front Doors (see No. 7) are the main entrance to the home and should be treated with the utmost care and respect. Scratches around the key holes are an ugly and tell-tale sign of sloppiness and lack of caring. There are so many door styles, so be careful in making sure that the style of the door is true to the style of the home. The paint colour and the wood finish can always be a little bit of a statement as this is an important part of the home.

Feng Shui teaches us that the Chi: the energy of our life force enters through here and it is important and should be treated as so.

Front doors should look like they care.
They should look happy and welcome one into a residence

No. 45 Front Door Hardware is always best to be a little large and more important as it is the gateway to the home.

Stay true to the homes style and allow the door to work well with the other elements but by using a larger fixture and maybe adding a knocker or a nice bell, the overall presentation of the initial first impression will be noticed.

Knobs and Knockers are a fun way to bring back yesteryear and announce that a home has style and class.

There is nothing like the sound a big brass or iron door knocker makes to announce a guests' arrival. It's your chance to brand your personality to your door.

Doorbell buttons are so inexpensive and it bothers me to see a cheap plastic one at the entrance to a home.

There are many types in the $30-80.00 range that all look much better and definitely make more of a statement then white plastic. Because I messed with Texas in my molding comments, to all Texans, I show thee this Texas door-bell plate with love.

For our 4 legged friends there are even dog touch bells

No. 46 Cabinet Hardware

Knobs and hardware technically are a part of the homes architecture as they are truly built in and are a fixed part of the property. Cabinet hardware need not be expensive, and should be placed in the right location on the cabinet, and be in a complimentary finish with other metals or wood in the home.

In larger kitchens and closets, nicer hardware can get pricey especially if you need 40 at $50.00 each, so be careful to choose wisely and appropriately.

Perhaps the most decadent thing I ever did was to install gold and clear crystal

Sherle Wagner knobs at the former Beverly Hills closet of the late Milton Berle. The heavenly knobs were $225.00 each and we needed 38. That's $8,550.00 plus tax, freight and installation please.

Decadent Sherle Wagner, Sphere Rock Crystal door Knob in antique gold finish, also available in Malachite with a Butler's silver finish.

Favorites of the Sultan of Brunei and used on all his private plane toilets. Leona Helmsley's private Boudoir bathrooms (I'm dating myself). Joan Collins and anyone else who can afford such insanely lavish cabinet jewelry.

No. 47 Electrical Outlets & Switches

Make sure that the switches and outlets are all the same colour and match in style. Nothing is more unsightly than a light switch in almond with a white back plate. Any odd jobs-man can switch out plates and one can even do it themselves. Although please don't ask me as I would electrocute myself. Take pictures of each different type on your phone and make a count before heading out to the hardware store. In bathrooms, kitchen back splashes and center islands it is very acceptable to have a colored switch that will help blend in with a wall or marble color. Stainless plates and light grey look sharp in contemporary kitchens.

Painted plates. Not a good look as they without fail will scratch and look like crap in no time. A switch is a switch is a switch so let's keep it real please and not try to hide the obvious. Oh and did I say clean. I am amazed how many filthy switches I see. A good maid or housekeeper should be able to manage that simple task. If not then wipe it yourself you will feel like you did something good.

Not a good look my dear.
Replace all switches and outlets so they match and are not dirty

No. 48 Windows, Window Frames and Glass

Again cleanliness is important, make sure that all window panes are cleaned and free from paint and dirt on both sides.

Peeled and chipped paint is NOT acceptable and screams renovation dollars needed.

Even if it means sanding and painting, windows must appear clean and be painted nicely.

Often just a good scrub will make a window frame look great. Also, make sure they all open as during inspection of a home this will be discovered.

No. 49 Closets & Storage Rooms should be wiped clean and have a fresh coat of paint. Shelves should be fixed to the walls and be clean. If there are no shelves in a closet at least try to have 2 or 3 installed. You can measure and they can pre-cut shelves in most hardware stores and installation is easy for any handyman.

Basically, when you open a closet door it should look like you would want to put your clothes or towels in it. Again, smell is important. If the closet smells musty wipe walls with an anti-bacterial and leave an air fresher inside.

His n His closet design I designed recently in Malibu

Lastly, closets are for storage of items and not people. I am so glad I came out of mine.

No. 50 Female Shoe Temples or Shoe Shrines

as they are commonly known, should pay homage to the art of the shoe. A home with even a small area that can be designated as a shoe sanctuary is sure to win over the heart of any woman and can possibly push a sale forward.

Correct lighting, preferably under shelf LED is best so it doesn't create heat and damage expensive leathers. A small chandelier or a pendant style fixture hanging from the ceiling will push light down onto the divine shoes as they are taken off the shelf and admired lovingly before being placed on her feet.

Seating placing a small stool, bench or chair if there is room close to hallowed shoe shelving is always a nice touch so one can be seated while putting the shoe on. Not so necessary with slip on pumps but with gladiators, laced boots or rollerblades, it's always nice to be able to put them on comfortably before marching, or rolling out of the closet.

Shelving should always be adjustable as usually space in a hallowed shoe closet is always at a premium. I advise clients to do a seasonal switch so that taller boots can be closer at hand in winter and sandals and flats can be close by and easy to reach for in summer.

The ultimate girls' dream is of course Mariah's 1,000 pair shoe closet. Thankfully we can achieve the slightest suggestion in a 3' wide section with simple white shelving and good lighting.

Any woman will say thank you.

No. 51 Air Conditioning/Heating Vents, Grilles & Registers

A great architectural statement can be made by just acknowledging that these all important mechanical outlets are there. They keep us warm in the winter and cool in the heat of summer. Firstly, as with everything they should be wiped clean. If you can see inside the duct and it has a white spray from a careless builder it's easy to spray the inside of the ducts with a black matte spray paint. This alone seriously looks so fabulous and chic I can't understand why everyone doesn't do it.

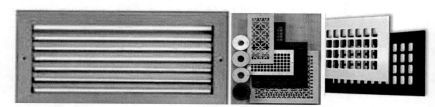

Regular Vent

Decorative Vents celebrate a home's style and elevate a design presence.

In higher end residences where in main room's vents are clearly visible, I always like to use a proper register grill, they come in all metal finishes and are paintable. A basic vent is $30-40 and a nice decorative one maybe $80-90 in the same size. In living areas and entry ways where you see vents or in floors, I like to get these changed as it sure makes a house feel like a home and adds richness to a home's architectural feel. In homes built before the 70's nice grilles existed. Sadly now everything needs to be made on the cheap and for the cheap so it has sadly become normal to see ugliness in common vents.

No. 52 Stairs Hand-rails, spindles, risers, treads and what not. Stairs are our way of getting between floors. They take more wear and tear than normal parts of our home as we trudge up and down them with regularity.

In general all areas of a staircase from floor to walls takes a beating. Again, cleanliness is the golden rule. Make sure the treads and risers are clean also the hand rails and spindles. If you have a wood tread on the stairs and a painted riser make sure that the riser has a fresh coat of semi-gloss or satin paint so it looks clean and can be easily wiped. Our feet and shoes bang up against risers so they need to be watched for scuffs.

Carpet runners should not show wear, if so replace with new carpet. Accent the rails by painting them a colour like brown or black satin depending on a home's décor as this can make a statement and pull an area together.

A contrasting or bright pattern will give a stairway greater presence.

No. 53 Lighting & Light Fixtures

It is crucial that from the outside through the inside a homes' lighting fixtures remain cohesive and in the same style and finish. Many times during the lifecycle of a home light fixtures are changed and added. The result is usually a mish mash of styles and not a good look.

Do a fixture count and take pictures of what is where to jog your memory. You will be surprised. Sometimes you can move existing fixtures around. I'll never forget walking into a condo in Miami once and in the back bedroom was this bloody amazing mid-century light hanging all alone, a total gem of a find. I had it relocated to the dining area alcove where it was clearly visible from the front door. It instantly became a free focal point in an otherwise dreary alcove.

George Kovacs is a genius modern day lighting designer. His designs are versatile and prices reasonable. Can you see how these fixtures tell a cool contemporary, fresh, sexy and exciting design story in a contemporary home?

By having all lighting coordinate from one or two vendors only, it immediately brings a sense of style that runs throughout the home and gives a better appearance.

No. 54 Basements should not feel like you are entering a scene in a horror movie or the Amityville house. If they are unfinished as many are, it's a great shame and something must be done before placing a home on the market.

It is a known fact that a finished basement adds many more dollars to a home. If they have a separate outside entrance and can be legally occupied and rented then they are a positive asset and should be treated with huge importance. If they are entered through the inside of a home then they still provide significant additional space which everyone likes to have.

Make sure there is no water intrusion and no smell of damp or rot as these are killers and buyers see dollar signs instantly. If they are unfinished, then make them clean and spotless, free from trash, cobwebs, dead rodents and insects. Essentially an unfinished basement can still be viewed as an asset only if it is spic and span.

With adequate lightings and ventilation. If there are any windows or natural light please ensure they are clean and in operable condition.

If there is a solid door from the exterior then switch the door to a French door and you instantly will get an abundance of light. Make sure there are just a few ceiling lights in the space so that at the flick of a switch the space becomes well-lit and a proud asset.

No. 55 Attics again seem to be neglected and much like basements are the scene of many horror movies.

Additional space is always needed and whether you can stand in, slide in or occupy an attic it is always a positive if any part of it can be used. It is relatively very inexpensive to have plywood installed on the rafters so that additional storage can be had.

As always speak with a qualified contractor to ensure that this can be done without disturbing the integrity of the joists. Always make sure there is an adequate light even if it is just a bulb so that the potential buyers can see up inside.

Remember when they buy the house they are also buying the attic. Having easy ladder access to the attic for storage is always a great idea to have

No. 56 Sides of a Property

Always walk an entire property and be aware of its surroundings.

Again, all areas must be clean and free from rubbish. Many times I look out from a ground floor window and see nooks or crannies outside the window that just beg for attention.

Recently at one of my Beverly Hills listings I noticed that the house was surrounded by a 5'-0" retaining wall that sat only 5'-0' away from the house. I told the client to place some landscaping outside each window as it was at eye level when you walked into the rooms. In this case we used decorative grasses and upon entering each room you saw this attractive arrangement of foliage at eye level outside.

One window had sliding door so I placed a small bistro table and 2 chairs with a plant pot in the corner and 2 solar lights.

It was nothing really special at all but it created the illusion of space and yet another area to use in the home, thus adding more value.

No. 57 Back Gardens and Yards are a

chance for us to celebrate nature and our mother earth that we are rapidly ruining. We all need a place to hide and a place to run to, a sanctuary.

The open land that surrounds properties is our gardens and yards, land I believe should be treated with respect and tended to. Our need to bring the outside in and have somewhat of a view from inside our dwellings stems from the basic fact that we are designed to live outside. Never ignore the rear of a property. The more that you can do with land that surrounds a home, the better.

Ultimately time and money dictate all that we do on a property, but keeping land in good order is very important. Always make sure native species are used so that you don't need to use water and they will grow naturally, thus meaning they will NOT need your time.

Gone are the days of **lawns and roses** in the desert. I can never understand that it is allowed in Palm Springs or Las Vegas when a plethora of cactus, succulents, grasses, shrubs and trees that are native in the deserts are not used.

Try to make an effort with at least a few natural groupings of God's given native species close to the windows of the back of a home. It will make the world of difference when a potential buyer looks outside the window.

No. 58 Artwork and Wall Hangings

Correct heights to install artwork are important as art is at our eye level. General rule of thumb is not to go above the line of the top of doors. In fact by keeping all artwork at the same height or same series of height lines throughout a home the eye will be more relaxed and it will bring a calm sense or architectural order to any interior.

With regards to subject matter and colour of art, it is subjective and I could write an entire thesis on my theories of what should and should not be used in a home but we in the end must work with what is given.

Please refrain from hanging personal pictures on the wall. It is only ok to do so on one wall in one area. Offices and hallways near bedrooms are OK.

When we walk clients through a home it is hard to imagine living in a home when it is a shrine to someone else's life. Politely ask your client to remove large family pictures and portraits as they add nothing nutritionally to a home's value.

My favourite street in the world is in Ipanema facing Leblon. Oh to walk down those sidewalks like the boy from Ipanema does every day.

A Brazilian art curator in Rio de Janeiro once asked me "Why Americans plaster their walls with pictures of themselves in such a blatantly vain manner". She also added "while South Americans and Caribbean's' adorn their walls in original oils and objects d' art".

Interesting take on cultures but very important to know that pictures of oneself and family all over a home are a no-no when one is trying to sell it.

No. 59 Clutter is never a good look. Even the tidiest of homeowners can be guilty of personal clutter. By this we mean excessive pictures of family (see item No. 58), books all over the place, personal items, hobby/arts 'n' crafts projects, kids toys around the house, which should not be seen.

Clutter or Clean? My living room (right) Kuala Lumpur, circa 2009

We as realtors need to politely speak with our clients about tidying up and removing clutter.

Thankfully, with the advent of HGTV and all of the popular shows that have brought to light the necessity of a clutter free home, these conversations are easier to have.

Bringing in some decorative boxes that items can be placed into and kept shelved is a much better look. These can be labeled and are still easy to access if on a shelf in an interior room or better yet in a closet.

No. 60 Laundry Rooms are an easy way to get big bonus points with female buyers. Even if it is only a laundry closet it should have as much shelving as possible, cool and adequate lighting and good flooring.

I like to paint the walls in a slightly different light colour and hang some fun poster art if there is room. There is no need to do a floor change to something less costly in a laundry area or room as nothing looks worse than an obvious cheap floor coming off a nice stone or wood floor. Generally Laundry rooms are small in size and the square footage should NOT break your floor budget.

Try to keep with re-occurring themes in the house so that the laundry room is a happy area to be in. This is definitely a room where cheap and cheerful can always reign sureme.

No. 61 Wig Rooms please don't laugh, I have done one. A wig room or wig closet should be given the same dignity and respect of a shoe closet.

The heads should have enough room and the lighting should be directed onto the shelving so the wigs will look their best.

Often an entertainer will want the outfit and jewelry to be hanging underneath the wig as it makes for easy packing for those busy on the road trips.

No. 62 Disco Rooms are probably the most decadent and can also easily cohabit with a gymnasium as they both share the same need of a wood floor or smooth vinyl. Mirrors that are required in the gym are also excellent surfaces to reflect the disco lights. Disco balls are an essential ingredient for a disco room and are available in a ceiling mounted box that opens and allows the ball to come down. Where height is an issue the disco ball can be easily mounted on a simple wall bracket and the magical reflections will still be able to travel across the room. It may appear slightly distorted but with all the dancing, being a little distorted is possibly a good thing.

Coloured lights are easy to order and install and there is a huge variety to choose from online. You will be surprised that just one disco light bar with a red, yellow and green flash light can be enough to create a traffic jam on any home dance floor. There should be a wet bar in the room as dancing without a drink can be an odd experience. Music is so easy to bring in to any room and I recommend a brand like Sonos as you can have speakers placed all over the house.

No. 63 Gift Wrapping Rooms are no longer

for the wealthy and privileged. We must give thanks to our dear friend Candy Spelling, who single handedly has done more for the gift wrapping industry with her decadent gift wrapping room than Martha Stewart at a Christmas wrap off for Macy's.

One can easily make part of an open closet into a wrapping area if space is a challenge. Go online and select your favorite papers, buy the roll holders and install them under shelves.

Be sure to get a few boxes, one for ribbons, one for bows, and always keep an assortment of small gift cards for notes in their own box. Tape, glue gun and scissors are also a must.

No. 64 Gyms are wonderful to have in a home however should always have an outside window element to them. Having a gym without natural light and more specifically a view of a lawn or outside is not the optimal. A wall mounted TV is a great way to keep you entertained and focused. Again a Sonos or similar type of music system will keep you biking, running or pumping.

This home gym above is perfectly lit and has adequate equipment

Flooring should not be carpet. Stay with wood and vinyl for wipe-ability and cleaning. There are also gym mats available in squares that can be placed together so that falling weights will not ruin the floor and give you a little bounce while standing on them. Make sure a ceiling fan is installed for optimum cooling and as always have a good light for those early morning or late night work outs.

Techno Gym is my favourite home gym system as its all built into the wall and comes in several styles. All so good looking that they can be on display in a main room and not relegated to a back room, thus making workouts more fun

No. 65 Faucets can make or break a bathroom design. They are so readily available, so easy to install and so crucial to improving the look and feel of a bathroom. Things you need to know about when buying a faucet which come in several different types.

Single-hole faucet as the name implies has one hole drilled in the counter that allows both the hot and cold feeder lines to be contained within it. I like the ease of being able to control the temperature with just a slight movement. I'll never go back to 2 faucets again, ever

3-hole faucets and the faucet spread 6", 8" or 12". Measure the distance from the centre of each faucet to faucet and this will give you "the spread". Many times the hot and cold water lines are flexible and will fit any size pre drilled holes but please always measure.

Wall and Deck Mounted Faucets. Most faucets are deck (counter mounted). However in the latter part of the 20th century, in its last decade, we saw a huge rise in the use of wall mounted faucets. They are available in single and 3-hole faucets and guess what? I don't like them.

They are a bitch to use and are usually used in combination with vessel (bowl) sinks. They make a splashy wet mess and I feel if they must be used, use them only in a powder room so you don't have to deal with a mess all the time.

No. 66 Shower Heads & Controls

The hallowed rain shower will give you more bang for your buck than any other bathroom item besides a faucet. Who doesn't like a rain shower? They make us feel good and are so easy to install that even I can do it.

Beware of shower heads that are larger than a 5" diameter. What tends to happen is that when you have a larger rain head the standard plumbing pipe will not deliver enough water and pressure wise you end up with a trickle. Remember older homes were not designed for these newer ideas that were not here 30 years ago.

Large shower heads used in new construction and renovations have 1" water lines that deliver a lot more flow per minute to the head and give a stronger flow for the larger head.

In these times of water scarcity it is really unnecessary and somewhat gluttonous to willingly use double the amount of water per shower than us common folk do. Don't you think?

No. 67 Glass shower enclosures vs. Shower curtains

In standard bathrooms that have a tub shower combo it is so inexpensive to buy a sliding clear glass door that sits on the tub. Make sure that the metal finish you use is the same as the faucets.

If a shower curtain must be used due to budget constraints, please, please, please do not go crazy with colours or the print. Remember to keep it simple. We want the bathroom to have some personality but simple stripes or a complimentary colour to the walls is all one needs.

Softer colours usually look best in smaller spaces as the curtain will be at eye level, so lighter grays, creams, whites and pale blues 'n' greens are all acceptable.

No. 68 Toilets & Thrones

should never be cracked or have loose seats, in general a toilet should look new. There are a plethora of toilets out there and I would find the one that suits the style of the bathroom and the budget. It is very inexpensive to have a toilet removed and replaced so there is really no excuse for this most wonderful of man's inventions to ever be looking anything but shiny and new.

Avoid coloured toilets like the plague. It is impossible to keep a coloured toilet looking clean and black is the worst. Close seconds are pink, blue and green. It is a nice departure from white when a light grey or light beige is used. These are the only colour substitutes that I recommend besides our much loved white latrines.

Solid White Marble Toilet with 24 carat gold leaf, hand carved clam shell wooden cover. Oprah had two in her "his and her's" powder rooms at her Fisher Island, Miami Apartment

Closing Words

Deferred Maintenance.

Want to be a smart realtor and try something new that will keep you in contact with your clients after they move in?

After your client closes on a new home, I advise doing a walk thru and itemize every item that could be upgraded to make the property more valuable when they list it for sale in the future. This way clients can have a convenient list that they can tackle at their own leisure.

Let's say for example there are 12 items on the list and one item can be done per month. In one year after taking ownership they are completed and everything on the list is done. This is important as it keeps you the agent on the mind of the buyer and when they are ready to make a move or another purchase you will clearly be on their mind. It also gives you a great reason to periodically check up on them and ask how the list is going. It shows you are genuinely interested in how the house is being maintained.

When listing a house we all know that the deferred maintenance list can seem daunting to sellers. So why not start the process at the beginning of ownership? The best part about having a "to do" list is that the new homeowner actually get to enjoy living in their new home and reaps all the benefits of the new changes while they are living there.

I cannot tell you how many clients rush to prepare their homes for sale, spend all this money on presentation and do not get to enjoy living in the house they upgraded as it gets sold.

The end

I hope that you have enjoyed the read and that you have found these tips both educational and funny. If anyone has taken offense to anything that I have said please know that without humor we are truly nothing.

"It is man's ability to poke fun at oneself that makes our journeys all the more worthwhile."

Enjoy the knowledge that I have shared with you and I look forward to you implementing these tips in your clients' homes for now and always.

If you take nothing else with you on your journey, I'd like you to remember these two powerful statements:

"Taking pride in ownership of property does not cost a thing"

"Cleanliness is after all next to godliness".

Foot notes: Attention my lovely American readers. Certain words are spelled the correct English way as this book is available globally to non-American English speaking cultures and people

Special thank you and love going out to:

My fabulous mummy **Marlene** for giving me life and raising me so well and my step father **Paul** for his loving support.

My daddy **Stuart Livingstone** who died at 44 in front of my eyes when I was 17.He never got to see all I've done. I have never had a father to ask how to do anything. I made mistakes as we all do but cannot help but wonder what how he would have guided me through life.

My maternal grandma **Rachel**, whose story telling ability, spirit and humor I got. Her strong belief in god and of knowing that the ones we lose stay close to us, is the very glue that holds me together.

My beautiful sister **Karen** who I lost tragically in July 2013. She was the first person I called as I got my real estate license. She screamed so loud with happiness and pride down that phone line from Florida. You are with me every second of every day. Karen and I miss you so much, like the deserts miss the rain. There is a gaping hole in my heart that can never, **ever, ever** be filled.

My beautiful 2 nieces **Samantha** and **Jessica** whom I love to the moon and stars and back. I encourage them to do what they love to do and to reach for their dreams always and to make their mummy proud.

My lovely Auntie **Gloria June Black** who edited the book with me. We combined the right English and American phrases along with my own unique Barrie-ism style of talking and writing.

Last but not least, the 10.8 lb. little boy who has my heart.

My beautiful Italian Greyhound Rio, whom I am madly and deeply in love with He fills my days with joy & love & is my constant companion since 2005.

Follow, find or contact Barrie at any of these places.

Use **#68bybarrie** when referring to the book in any social media.

Twitter: @barrieinla

Instagram: @barrieinla

**Facebook: Barrie Livingstone Design
&
Barrie Livingstone Real Estate**

www.barrielivingstone.com

Made in the USA
Middletown, DE
22 May 2016